'Know the Game' Series

MOTOR CYCLING

CONTENTS

Printed in Great Britain by *Terry & Nephew Ltd., Wesley Street, Dewsbury, Yorks.*

FOREWORD

To know your game is the longest single step along the road towards deriving whole hearted enjoyment from it, and I am indeed pleased to recommend this little volume to the newcomer to motorcycling. Some older hands, too, will find it extremely informative and helpful.

I like especially the order of its chapters. So many motorists of today drive around with only the sketchiest idea of how their mechanical progress is started, controlled or maintained. No motorcyclist need continue in this state of ignorance for I refuse to believe that it is blissful, particularly when the occasinal spot of bother occurs. To know how the motorcycle works in the way this book explains, that is, not too technically, will assist our newcomer, who may not have purchased a new machine, to keep it on the road.

The same simple, straighforward method of setting down and advising on all the aspects of our sport, even to the most suitable types of clothing to wear, is pursued throughout the book and in the hands of the present day motorcyclist it cannot fail to ensure that he "knows the game" and enjoys it. To keep absolutely up to date with events he should read at least one of the motorcycling journals and join a Club. In the latter he will, unless he is a queer bird, inevitably find much pleasure in the company of fellow enthusiasts for the greatest sport of all.

Chairman, Auto-Cycle Union.

THE MOTOR CYCLE AND ITS COMPONENTS

1. Front tyre
2. Internal expanding brake in full width hub
3. Telescopic front fork
4. Front mudguard
5. Headlamp, containing speedometer
6. Steering head
7. Fuel tank
8. Knee grips
9. Engine
10. Exhaust pipe
11. Timing case containing magneto and dynamo drives
12. Centre stand
13. Pillion footrests
14. Carburettor
15. Dual seat
16. Oil tank with matching tool box on other side
17. Chain guard
18. Swinging fork
19. Rear spring unit
20. Rear hub with sprocket on other side
21. Silencer
22. Rear mudguard with lifting handles
23. Rear number plate with built-in lamps

Fig. 1.

The publishers wish to acknowledge the help given to them by B.S.A. Motor Cycles Ltd. in providing some of the illustrations used.

The Motor Cycle

At first glance, a motor cycle may appear to be almost deceptively simple. In actual fact, it is a fine example of precision engineering, with much compressed into a relatively small space, and with power and durability coupled to the minimum of weight. A big touring motor cycle, for example, may weigh little more than 400 lb., yet its engine often develops more power than that of a medium-sized family touring car. Fig. 1 shows a 500 c.c. machine with the most important components indicated.

Engine

Unlike cars, which are usually classified according to a horsepower formula, motor cycles are identified with the actual cubic capacity of their engines. Thus a "125" is a machine with a cylinder capacity in the 125 c.c. class; a "650" one with an engine approaching 650 c.c. Normally, engines are made slightly below the capacity limits to allow the cylinders to be renovated by slight boring-out without taking the machine into a higher capacity (and, perhaps, a higher tax!) class. For this reason, the "125" will usually be of about 123 c.c., and the "650" of about 646 or 649 c.c. capacity.

"Capacity", of course, refers to the amount of petrol/air mixture which the engine can draw in during one single downward stroke of the piston, and it is, in fact, also a fair guide to the power of the engine.

There are two main types of engine — the four-stroke and the two-stroke. In most respects, they are of similar construction. A pair of flywheels or cranks form the crankshaft, which is carried inside the crankcase. An offset pin on the flywheels — the crankpin — carries the connecting rod, which in turn carries the piston.

The piston fits snugly inside the cylinder, or barrel, which is closed at the top by the cylinder head. This is the basic layout of all piston engines.

To understand the working principle it is best to begin with **the four-stroke cycle** — so called because the piston makes four strokes (journeys up or down the cylinder) in completing it (Fig. 2).

Imagine the piston at the top of the cylinder (top dead centre). As it travels down it lowers the pressure inside the cylinder, enabling petrol/air mixture to be drawn in when a valve in the head is opened. This is the induction stroke (Fig. 2a).

As it reaches the end of its travel (bottom dead centre) the valve is closed and the mixture trapped. The piston rises again, and steadily compresses the mixture — a necessary operation, since it will burn properly only when compressed. This, then, is called the compression stroke (Fig. 2b).

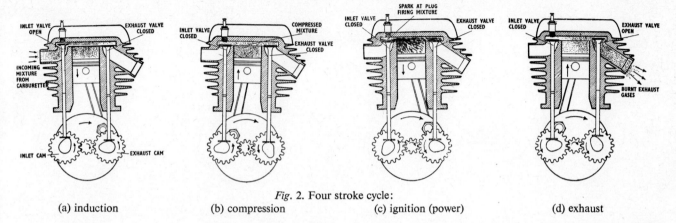

Fig. 2. Four stroke cycle:

(a) induction   (b) compression   (c) ignition (power)   (d) exhaust

Now comes the power stroke (Fig. 2c). The piston approaches top dead centre, and a spark is made to jump across the points of a sparking plug fixed into the head. The petrol/air mixture burns rapidly and consequently expands, thrusting the piston down the cylinder again.

Lastly comes the exhaust stroke (Fig. 2d). The piston rises in the bore; another valve in the head opens, and the burned mixture is expelled. On the next down stroke of the piston, fresh mixture will be drawn in, and a new cycle will have commenced.

With the four-stroke, then, the sequence is induction, compression, power, exhaust. It is possible so to design an engine, however, that these strokes are to some extent combined, so that the engine fires whenever the piston comes to the top of its stroke. Engines of this type are called two-stroke engines and **the two-stroke cycle** is shown in Fig. 3. Though simpler, mechanically, than the four-stroke, this type of unit is more difficult to understand, since there are always two things happening at once.

Assume that the piston of a two-stroke engine is at the bottom of its stroke. Two separate operations will just have taken place. Burned gas will have escaped through a hole (port) in the wall of the cylinder, and two streams of fresh gas will have rushed through two more such ports leading from the crankcase into the cylinder (transfers).

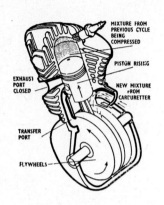 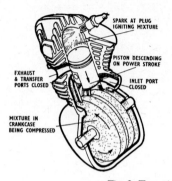 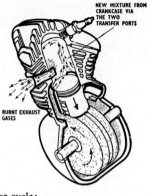 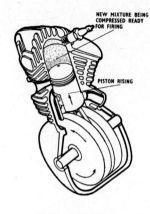

Fig. 3. Two stroke cycle:

(a) compression/induction   (b) power stroke/compression   (c) exhaust/transfer   (d) cycle restarts

The piston now rises. First, it closes the two transfer ports. Then it closes the exhaust port. Its further movement compresses the mixture (Fig. 3a).

It is still rising. Its bottom edge (skirt) uncovers yet another port (induction) through which mixture streams into the crankcase, which is made specially gas-tight so that it can be used in this way. At the top of the stroke a spark occurs; the mixture ignites, and the piston is pushed down the cylinder on a power stroke. Immediately, it covers the induction port, and begins to compress the mixture now trapped in the crankcase (Fig. 3b).

As it nears the bottom of its stroke its top edge uncovers the exhaust port, and the burned gases rush out into the exhaust pipe (Fig. 3c). A split second later the piston uncovers the transfer ports and the fresh charge is pumped into the cylinder (Fig. 3d).

These, then, are the two strokes of the two-stroke engine: downwards stroke is power in the cylinder, compression in the crankcase; upwards stroke is compression in the cylinder, induction in the crankcase. The exhaust stroke is absent, being combined into the dying moments of the power stroke, with the transfer period occurring immediately afterwards. Reference to Figs. 2 and 3 will make the exact details of both systems quite clear.

At first glance, it might seem that a two-stroke engine should give twice as much power as a four-stroke engine of equal capacity, for it has twice the power strokes in a given time. In actual fact it normally develops slightly *less* power than a four-stroke, since it is impossible to prevent some of the burned gas remaining in the cylinder, and to prevent some of the fresh charge slipping out of the still-open port which — since it opened first — closes last. And at high engine speeds, there is insufficient time to transfer a full charge anyway.

For this reason, the two-stroke's superiority in theory is absent in practice, save at relatively low engine speeds where it does, in fact, develop more pulling power (torque) than the four-stroke. Its greatest advantage is, of course, simplicity. The four-stroke must have valves in the cylinder head. It needs springs to hold them shut, cams, rockers or push-rods to open them; timing gear to ensure that they open and close at the right moment. The two-stroke has simple ports built into the cylinder, and works efficiently with just three moving parts — the piston, connecting rod and crank assembly. It is also a much smoother engine when running, equivalent to a twin-cylinder four-stroke.

Carburettor

To function, an engine needs certain ancillaries. It must have some means of converting the petrol in the tank into a petrol/air mixture which will burn in the cylinder. This is done by a carburettor (Fig. 4) — little

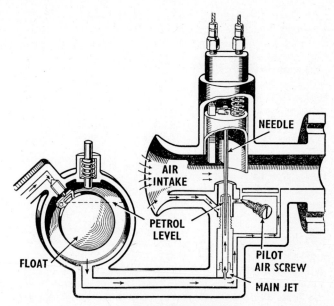

Fig. 4. The carburettor

more, in principle, than a glorified scent-spray. Fuel is fed from the tank to a chamber on the carburettor known as the float chamber. This contains a simple float and needle valve assembly which cuts off the fuel when the chamber is full and opens as soon as the level falls, rather like the ball cock assembly in the domestic cistern. From the float chamber, the petrol passes through an internal passage into a well, in which is a tube with a fine metering hole known as a jet. The other end of the tube projects into the choke — the central passage of the carburettor, through which air passes on its way to the cylinder. As the air rushes over the end of the tube it sucks up small droplets of petrol, which emerge in the form of a fine spray. By varying the relative sizes of the jet and the choke, the correct petrol/air mixture of roughly 14 parts of air to one of petrol, by weight, can be obtained.

Such a carburettor as this, though, would only enable the engine to run at one speed. To make variations of engine speed possible a throttle control is added. This must be of a design which keeps the petrol/air ratio constant, and thus it must operate both on the choke and the jet. It does this quite simply. The amount of air entering is controlled by a slide which can be moved up and down in the choke. It has a needle attached to it, and this moves up and down in the tube carrying the jet. Thus, as the supply of air is increased or decreased by the slide, the supply of petrol is altered accordingly by the needle.

Carburettors normally have provision for over-riding the set proportion when a rich mixture is needed for starting the engine. Sometimes a "strangler" is used, which is a sliding or rotating cover which reduces the air supply, while leaving the petrol unaltered. On larger models a similar function is performed by an additional air slide, usually operated by a bowden control. There is also a "bleed" from the jet to a point behind the throttle slide through which a small amount of petrol can pass. This is called the pilot jet, and its purpose is to provide for a supply of petrol when the engine is merely idling. Finally, the air entering the modern instrument is usually cleaned first by means of a filter, which helps to prevent the smooth working surfaces of the piston and bore from being scratched by microscopic, but very hard, fragments of stone which form a proportion of the dust normally found in the air.

Electrical System

The electrical side of the motor cycle can be made up in various ways. For many years the most popular arrangement was to have a separate magneto to provide current for the ignition system, and a separate dynamo to recharge the battery which feeds the lights. This type of installation is still widely employed, but the use of a single electrical generator is becoming more and more popular. On two-strokes, the flywheel magneto-generator — a dual purpose instrument in which the actual flywheel of the engine is utilised as part of the generator — is universally employed, and even on bigger machines the alternating current type of generator is gaining ground.

The principle is the same, however, in all cases. For ignition of the fuel, a high tension current is made to travel down the ignition lead. This current is of an intensity sufficient to enable it to jump the gap between the plug points in the form of a spark, thereby firing the charge in the combustion chamber. Production of this high tension current depends upon the action of what is virtually a mechanical switch incorporated within the magneto. Called a "contact breaker", it is controlled by a cam which opens and closes the points of the contact breaker at predetermined times. While the points are closed, electrical current is allowed to pass through the first of a series of long wire windings in another highly important component — the ignition coil. When the contact-breaker points are opened, the sudden breaking of the connection causes high tension current to be generated in a second set of windings which surround the first, but which are not directly connected to them. The result is the spark at the plug points. In a two-stroke engine, this action may take place 5,000 times each minute — an indication of the magnitude of the work which this basically simple device undertakes.

Some of the simpler motor cycles and scooters, and all mopeds, dispense with the use of a battery for lighting purposes, and rely upon the current fed straight from the generator to the lighting set. This system is known as "direct lighting". It is cheap and reliable, but has the disadvantage that the lights will work only when the engine is running. Sometimes a small dry battery, such as those used in cycle lamps, is incorporated to provide a parking light and thereby overcome this disadvantage. The larger motor cycles, however, use a wet battery — one in which acid and metal plates form the "storage"— to feed the lights and horn. In such a layout, the generator's job is to keep the battery fully charged.

Transmission and Gearbox

Although the speed of a motor cycle can be varied over fairly wide limits — from, say 750 r.p.m. to 5,750 r.p.m. — its power output is not constant, and it runs most efficiently within a certain narrow band on its rev. range. Just how great is this degree of flexibility depends upon the engine designer. He may have decided to sacrifice pulling power at low speed in favour of a high maximum speed — as he would, for example, in producing a racing engine. Had he been asked to produce a unit to power a family sidecar outfit, however, he would have reversed this procedure, and arranged for plenty of power at the lower engine speeds, coupled with a less ambitious performance at the upper end of the range. For an all-round club or touring model, he might choose to concentrate on the provision of good acceleration coupled with a moderately high cruising speed. But whatever formula the designer chooses, he inevitably has to compromise.

Not only does the internal-combustion engine produce its best performance within a narrow speed range, but this also varies from machine to machine. It would obviously be impossible to use a motor cycle which could run at, say, only 50-55 m.p.h. Hence the incorporation of a throttle control. But this, too, solves only part of the problem. To work at all, the engine must be geared down, so that the road wheels turn at a slower speed than the engine crankshaft. The internal-combustion engine, unlike a steam engine, cannot produce sufficient power at low speeds to enable a direct coupling to be made.

This single gear ratio might be ideal at 55 m.p.h., with the engine producing 5,000 r.p.m., but the machine would never be able to travel at less than 15 m.p.h. nor move away from a standstill. The solution is to use more than one ratio, by the provision of a gearbox.

The number of gears required depends to some extent on the job the machine has to do. Some racing machines have used gearboxes giving five or six speeds — indeed, many years ago there was a very famous motor cycle called the Rudge "Multi", which had a control system allowing up to 20 gear variations. Many mopeds, however, operate satisfactorily on two gears (some of the simplest, with a restricted performance, do in fact use a single gear), while the majority of scooters and motor cycles have three or four ratios.

In principle, a gearbox is simply a case containing a number of different combinations of gearwheels, any one of which can be selected at will (Fig. 5). First gear ("bottom") is used for moving off and climbing really steep gradients. Top gear is used for cruising. The remaining gears ("intermediates") give a greater concentration of engine effort for fast overtaking or for hill climbing, and enable the engine to run more happily when the machine is moving slowly in heavy traffic.

Gearboxes can either be entirely separate from the engine or may be built into a common housing in the rear of the crankcase. This latter form is known as "unit construction". A compromise between the two is to bolt an independent gearbox to the rear of the engine — "semi-unit" construction, in fact.

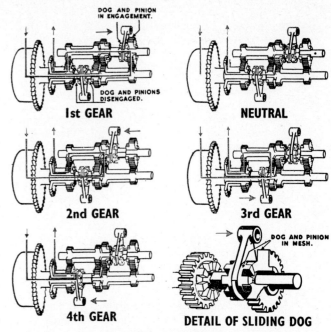

Fig. 5. The gearbox

A chain or a pair of gears normally form the "primary transmission", which carries the power from the crankshaft to the gearbox. This is also made into a reduction drive, so that the gearbox shaft turns at roughly half the rate of the crankshaft.

On the majority of machines the "secondary drive" from the gearbox to the rear wheel consists of a chain operating on sprockets. This, again, is a reduction drive. The sum total of these two speed reductions, plus the reduction which takes place inside the gearbox, in the case of the indirect ratios gives the overall gearing. This is expressed as a ratio — the number of crankshaft revolutions to one revolution of the rear wheel. The greater the crankshaft revolutions, the lower the gear. The lower the gear, the more pulling power is applied and the greater the load which can be overcome.

To take a typical example, a four-speed touring motor cycle might have overall ratios of around 5, 6, 8 and 13 to 1. Assuming that the effective range of the engine was from 2,000 to 5,000 r.p.m., bottom gear would give from 0-30 m.p.h., second from 19-48 m.p.h., third from 25-64 m.p.h. and top gear 32-78 m.p.h.

Each gear, obviously, overlaps by a substantial margin the gear above and below it, and it is up to the rider to make the best use of the flexibility so permitted. In this case, the engine might be operating at maximum torque efficiency at 3,500 r.p.m., so gear changes would be made at 20, 35, and 45 m.p.h. where the best use of the engine was desired. Many other factors enter into the calculation, however, for the correct use of the gears is one of the great arts of the motor cyclist and one which will be examined more fully in a later chapter.

Completing the transmission system is the clutch (Fig. 6). This is a simple friction device consisting of a number of plates held together by springs and mounted,

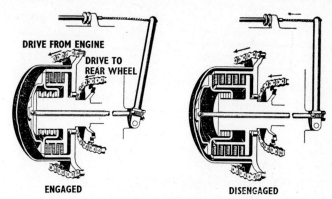

DRIVE FROM ENGINE

DRIVE TO REAR WHEEL

ENGAGED

DISENGAGED

Fig. 6. The clutch

alternately, either on the clutch body or on the clutch centre which is connected to the gearbox. There is no direct connection between the body and the centre. Normally, the plates form one solid body due to the spring pressure and transmit the drive, but when this pressure is released they separate. The plates attached to the body continue to revolve, but those on the clutch centre are no longer being driven. The load on the gearbox is thus eased, enabling a clean gearchange to be made. And, of course, the clutch also enables the drive to be taken up gradually when the machine is moving away from a standstill.

In the type of motor cycle considered here, with a two-stage reduction drive, the primary drive is usually enclosed in a case and runs in oil, while the secondary drive is left exposed or only partly shielded, though there has in recent years been an increasing movement towards rear chain cases as well.

A less common type of transmission is by shaft to bevel or worm gears in a rear wheel casing — rather like a car in miniature. This is used on some machines where the engine is mounted transversely — that is, with the flywheel across the frame, rather than in line with it. On such machines, the primary drive is usually eliminated, and the gearbox is bolted direct to the engine, with the clutch interposed.

Frames and Suspension

Motor cycle frames are usually constructed from steel tubing, although some manufacturers prefer to use steel pressings welded together. For many years, the normal motor cycle frame was basically similar to the diamond frame of the pedal cycle, with the rear wheel held in rigid rear stays. Nowadays, the duplex frame, with duplicated down-tubes, is more usual, and most machines have rear suspension.

Swinging-arm systems are the most generally accepted (Fig. 7). In these, the wheel is held in a more or less horizontal fork, pivoting on a substantial bearing on the main frame. A pair of spring units, usually containing hydraulic shock absorbers to prevent spring oscillation, is mounted on the swinging fork, with the tops connected to a sub-frame. This system gives the maximum of well-controlled movement and has proved thoroughly reliable in practice.

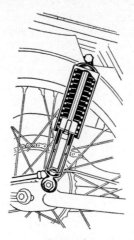

Fig. 7. Swinging-arm suspension

An alternative, though increasingly rare nowadays, is plunger suspension (Fig. 8). A spring plunger is incorporated into the rear frame, and the wheel spindle s mounted on sliders which can move up or down against the resistance of springs. Movement with this type of unit is limited, and the wheel spindle needs to be especially strong, since it must act as the link between the two independent plungers. One manufacturer — Triumph — produced an ingenious variant of this system some years ago in the form of a spring hub. This was basically a single plunger unit built into the rear hub, with a rigid spindle held in the rear stays. Other variants included the Ariel system, using short pivoted links in place of the simple plungers.

For front suspensions, telescopic forks (Fig. 9) are the most popular. These are basically similar to a plunger rear suspension system, but with a far longer and softer movement. Hydraulic damping is usually employed, save on mopeds and the smaller motor cycles.

The swinging-fork system has also been applied to front suspensions and it has found popularity on scooters.

Fig. 8
Plunger rear springing

Fig. 9
Telescopic forks

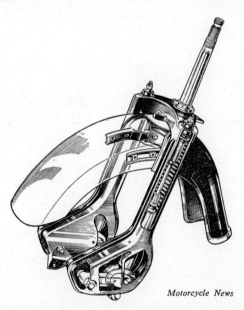

Motorcycle News

Fig. 10. A modern trailing link motor cycle fork, with pressed steel blades — in which the links, springs and dampers are totally enclosed. In this design the links trail behind their pivots.

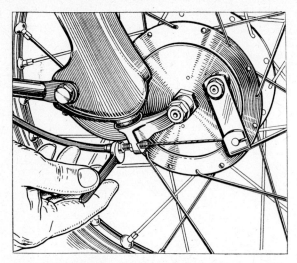

Fig. 11. Simple leading link forks, such as this, are popular on light scooters and mopeds

but for motor cycles it is used more often by Continental factories than by British manufacturers.

Link forks (Figs. 10 and 11) in which the wheel is carried on relatively short links rather than on long arms have increased their popularity in recent years, more especially in Italy, but are again more usually found on scooters. A hydraulically-damped link fork is, however, fitted to a number of British lightweight motor cycles of up to 250 c.c.

Brakes

Brakes are another facet of motor cycle design in which great progress has been made. Application of a brake causes friction, absorbing energy which would otherwise go to propelling the machine. The brake converts this energy into heat, which is dissipated into the surrounding air. Lining area, diameter and the heat-conducting qualities of the brake drum material are major factors in brake performance, although the real limiting factor is the adhesion of the tyres on the road surface.

Motor cycles normally use internal-expanding brakes, in which the action of a cam brings friction-lined shoes into contact with the face of a drum. Nowadays it is usual for this drum to be built into full-width hubs, often ribbed to increase the surface area and so aid heat dissipation. Brake diameters can range from as little as three or four inches on mopeds to as much as eight or nine inches on fast motor cycles.

Some form of mechanical control, either by rods or by cable, is used for motor cycle brakes, although experiments have been made with hydraulic operation. Coupled brakes, in which one pedal or lever operates both front and rear brakes, were tried some years ago, and have recently been re-introduced on mopeds. More usually, however, two-wheelers of all types retain the well-proved system of independent brake operation by hand for the front brake and by pedal for the rear.

CHOOSING A MACHINE
and LEARNING TO RIDE

ALTHOUGH there is a whole galaxy of machines on the market with engine capacities ranging from 50 c.c. up to 700 c.c., the learner-rider is not legally allowed to ride any solo machine with a capacity greater than 250 c.c. This guards against the beginner riding a machine that is too powerful for him to handle. This does not mean, however, that the small machine need be regarded merely as a stepping stone. In many cases, it is the best motor cycle for the job on its own merits alone.

The first step should be to form a clear opinion about the work the motor cycle is to do. If it is to be a pleasure machine, pure and simple, it is possible to accept the relatively high running costs of, say, a "650" without too much heart-burning. On the other hand, a machine which is going to form daily transport, and be a hobby as well, needs to have a fair degree of economy.

If the pleasure riding is to consist of short jaunts down to the coast no great speed is needed; on the other hand, weekly trips of two or three hundred miles call for more sustained speed than the average lightweight can provide.

The wise rider, then, will choose the smallest machine which will do the job. In most cases, this will be a model from the 150/250 c.c. range, giving a choice of single- or twin-cylinder machines in both two-stroke and four-stroke classes. These will tackle any task — save possibly that of sustained sidecar work, for which a "500" at least should be chosen — and combine this with the minimum running costs.

The choice between two-stroke and four-stroke is mainly one of personal whim. As a general rule, the two-stroke will be smoother and have better hill-climbing characteristics. It is also simpler to maintain. The four-stroke will have a slightly better performance, may be more economical; and is rather less fussy in its operation.

A multi-cylinder engine — and in this class the choice includes horizontally-opposed and vertical twin four-strokes — and vertical twin two-strokes — is normally smoother and responds to the throttle better than a single-cylinder engine. It may also have slightly more power. Complication, however, is doubled.

A vertical twin is an engine in which the cylinders are located side by side. With a four-stroke, the pistons rise and fall together to give an even firing interval which is exactly the same as that of a single-cylinder two-stroke. In a two-stroke twin, the pistons rise and fall alternately to give the same firing interval as could be obtained from a four-cylinder four-stroke. The horizontally-opposed twin has one cylinder protruding from each side of the crankcase. The firing interval is the same as that of the vertical twin, but its balance is almost perfect, and it is one of the smoothest running of all engines.

TOP LEFT

Fig. 12. Simplicity of layout characterises this 50 c.c. machine — a typical example of the "powered cycle" approach to moped design. It has neither gears nor suspension, though a clutch is fitted.

TOP RIGHT

Fig. 13. This 75 c.c. machine shows clearly the continental influence on modern lightweight motorcycle design.

BOTTOM LEFT

Fig. 14. An example of race-bred streamlining applied to a touring motor cycle to give weather protection.

Once the decision of engine type and capacity has been made, the rest of the specification must be decided upon. A spring frame, preferably of swinging-arm type, is more than a luxury nowadays. It offers so much in the way of comfort and added safety that it is more or less a necessity.

With machines up to 150 c.c. a three-speed gearbox is usually quite satisfactory — although, logically, the smaller engines should need more gears rather than less. Again, however, a four-speed gearbox is a wise investment if obtainable.

Proceeding in this way, and measuring each machine against your needs and against the purpose it is to fulfil it is possible to eliminate from the reckoning most of the possible models. A choice from the remainder must be made on different grounds — price, availability of service and spares, one's own judgment of the machine's practicability, workmanship, and so forth.

A second choice confronts the novice — whether to buy new or second-hand. A new machine, covered by a maker's guarantee, is a safe bet, of course, but it requires careful handling during the first 1,000 miles of its life to ensure that it is properly run in, and that everything settles down nicely. Mishandling at this stage could knock thousands of miles off its life, and pounds off its eventual resale value.

If a second-hand machine is decided upon, it must be in good condition. A veritable two-wheeled wreck may teach you a lot in a short time, but the lessons could be of the wrong sort. There are two guides to follow — the condition of the machine itself, with special reference to any signs of "chewed" nuts and bolts to indicate a careless previous owner — and the number of previous owners noted in the log-book. The more owners, the greater the chances that the machine has been mishandled. The ideal to aim at should be a model which is still current in production, not more than a year or 18 months old, with one previous owner and between 5,000 and 10,000 miles showing on the mileage recorder.

Before using a machine on the road, you must yourself be the holder of a provisional driving licence for Group 7 vehicles; the machine must bear a current licence disc; and you must be insured against third-party risks. This last point is vital — to drive without insurance is regarded as one of the most serious of motoring offences. This insurance does not cover the motor cycle itself — it covers the *driver* of the motor cycle (usually one named driver) against any legal claim which may be brought against him as a result of his driving. To cover the motor cycle, extra insurance has to be negotiated.

The normal cover is third party only, leaving the motor cycle itself uninsured. After this comes third party, fire and theft — which is self explanatory. Finally, you

TOP LEFT

Fig. 15. This well-known British scooter is unusually powerful with a twin cylinder 250 c.c. O.H.V. engine

BOTTOM LEFT

Fig. 16. In this 250 c.c. machine, a complete breakaway from traditional design has been made by using a pressed-steel box-member for the frame, enclosing the engine, and providing built-in weather protection

BOTTOM RIGHT

Fig. 17. A racing frame developed on a succession of top class T.T. motorcycles has been applied for road use in this powerful 650 c.c. machine.

Fig. 18. A 350 c.c. British motor cycle.

Fig. 19. Originating from a pre-war design, this 500 c.c. machine has been developed as an extremely successful super-sports model.

Fig. 20. A Japanese motor cycle typical of the type of machine which became extremely popular with younger riders — although only 250 c.c. it is capable of out-performing many 500 c.c. machines.

can obtain comprehensive insurance, which protects the rider and the machine against all normal risks. Naturally, comprehensive insurance is more expensive than the other types of cover, but on balance it is a wise investment.

Riding a motor cycle may not be covered by any life insurances you hold, and it is as well to check this point before actually riding a machine. Most insurance companies will accept motor cycle personal accident risks for an extra premium.

As soon as you acquire a used motor cycle, you must notify the change of ownership to the appropriate licensing authority, whose name can be found in the log-book.

It should also not be overlooked that the law requires a learner-rider to carry L-plates at all times until he passes the driving test. Until this has been done, any passenger carried must be a fully-qualified driver for vehicles of Group 7, and must have held his substantive licence for not less than two years.

The total cost of becoming a motor cyclist need not be prohibitively high, more especially when the machine itself can be bought on hire purchase. In terms of total cash, one could expect to obtain a good new or second-hand lightweight for around £130. Tax and insurance might account for another £20, and a sum kept in hand for spares and tyre replacements five more pounds on top of that. A minimum of riding kit would cost a further £12 and the driving test (allowing for loss of pay for an afternoon off work) perhaps a further £2, making a total of £169.

Running costs can be variously calculated since, strictly speaking, they should include an allowance for depreciation in the value of the machine, and for re-placement parts and so forth. In practice, the ordinary user is concerned solely with the cost of fuel and oil. Ready-mixed two-stroke fuel costs about five shillings per gallon, and most machines will average around 100 m.p.g., so allowing a figure of ¾d. per mile would cover not only fuel and oil, but gearbox oil changes and greasing as well.

CLOTHING and ACCESSORIES

EQUIPPING YOURSELF for motor cycling does not end merely with the buying of a machine. Motor cycling is an open-air sport, and even where windscreens or fairings are fitted the rider is more or less exposed to the elements. Good riding kit is a necessity.

The first essential is to buy a safety helmet (Fig. 21). Motor cycles, properly handled, are not dangerous, but the rider is more vulnerable than is a car driver, and the sensible man equips himself accordingly. The purpose of the helmet is to provide an insurance against a tumble, which can be caused by no fault of the rider himself. A swerve to avoid an incautious child, or negligence on the part of some other road-user, can bring a motor cyclist off his machine. It is mere common sense to ensure that the vulnerable human skull is properly protected against such a risk.

There is a wide range of helmets available, made to the requisite British Standard, which do their job well and which cost only a few pounds. It is important to select a helmet which fits snugly, and to wear it at all times when riding the machine — for short trips, as well as for long ones.

Fig. 21. A safety helmet is essential

Fig. 22.
Goggles with
safety glass are best

If you sustain a spill when wearing it, discard it, and buy another at once. It may have been weakened. In any case you should budget for a replacement every 18 months, since hair oil, sweat, and normal wear and tear gradually cause a helmet to deteriorate.

Equally essential is a good pair of goggles (Fig. 22). Even with windscreens, there is usually a certain amount of back-draught which can damage the eyes, and insects or stones thrown up by other vehicles could score an unlucky hit. Goggles with lenses of safety glass are best for all-round use — celluloid lenses usually become scratched and give poor night vision — and it is important to obtain a pair in which the frame moulds nicely to the face to exclude draughts.

The type of glove purchased will depend upon the equipment fitted to your machine. On a "streamliner", or one with extensive handlebar shielding, a fairly light pair will suffice. On a "naked" model, a pair of weather-flapped horsehide mitts with silk inners will give best service in winter, and a light pair of finger-type gloves will be needed for summer riding.

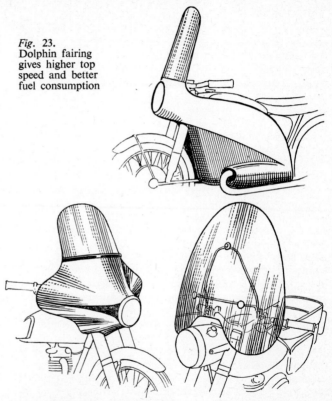

Fig. 23.
Dolphin fairing
gives higher top
speed and better
fuel consumption

Fig. 24. Windscreen incorporating
Handlebar

Fig. 25. Windscreen

The two-piece suit, either in plastics or proofed fabric, is the most popular riding kit today. It has the great advantage of flexibility, since the coat can be worn and the leggings carried on the machine during fine weather. Suits, however, are not usually as warm as the heavy riding coat, used in conjunction with rubber waders or proofed-fabric over-trousers. This latter combination is unquestionably the best for bad-weather use, so a possible compromise is to buy a two-piece suit and a riding coat, and to ring the changes between coat and jacket as the weather demands. For a foot covering, a short pair of rubber overboots is adequate and easy to pack away when not in use.

More and more riders are fitting fairings to their machines. Some years ago, the only method of building-in weatherproofing was to use a windscreen and leg-shields, which detracted from performance and appearance. Thanks to racing experience, however, there has now been developed the "dolphin" fairing (Fig. 23) which, besides incorporating all the protection which the old equipment could give, also gives a higher top speed and reduced fuel consumption. Some manufacturers produce machines with this equipment inbuilt, and for most others there are proprietary "dolphins" available. Full frontal streamlining is also made.

Windscreens, too, have undergone a revolution during the past decade. The latest designs incorporate efficient handlebar fairings (Fig. 24) which give excellent protection, and a slight performance bonus. The older type of screen (Fig. 25), with separate legshields, is, however, still popular on purely utility models.

Extra equipment which can be fitted to motor cycles covers a very wide range indeed. Luggage-carrying capacity can be increased by use of pannier sets (Fig. 26) and luggage grids. Protection against a spill is offered by crash bars. Spot- and fog-lamps can be added to ease

Fig. 26. Pannier set and luggage grid

driving at night, or under bad conditions. More powerful horns; direction indicator sets; multiple stop lamps; tank covers incorporating parcel space or map pockets; impervious seat covers; locking filler caps; embellishers and so forth are just a few of the other myriad items which the motor cycle accessories industry produces

Fig. 27. Correct riding position:

1. Adjust handlebars to give slight forward lean to body

2. Adjust handlebar angle to permit straight forearm and slightly angled upper arm. Elbows must be tucked in to side and forearms straight

3. Adjust riding position to give near right angle at knee joint. Knees must be snug against the tank

RIDING A MOTOR CYCLE

BEFORE TAKING a motor cycle on the road all the controls should be adjusted so that they fit the build of the rider Most machines, nowadays, have a dual seat which cannot be raised or lowered, but such components as footrests, gear and brake controls, handlebars and so forth can be positioned to suit the individual (Fig. 27).

The aim should be to make yourself as comfortable as possible, and to have each control where it can be used with the minimum expenditure of time and effort. Typical motor cycle and scooter handlebar controls are shown in Figs. 28 and 29.

Fig. 28. Motor cycle handlebar controls and instruments:

1. Clutch lever	6. Ammeter
2. Dummy twist grip	7. Speedometer
3. Ignition or air lever	8. Light switch
4. Horn button	9. Twist grip throttle
5. Dip switch	10. Front brake lever

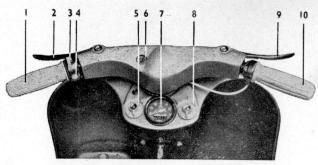

Fig. 29. Scooter handlebar controls and instruments:

1. Twist grip gear control	6. Handlebar lock
2. Clutch lever	7. Speedometer
3. Dip switch	8. Light switch
4. Horn button	9. Front brake lever
5. Ignition switch	10. Twist grip throttle

Adjust footrests so that the knees take up an angle which is either a right angle or slightly greater. A sharply bent knee restricts circulation. Where the handlebars are adjustable, position them so that the forearms are straight and the elbows close in to the sides when the hands are rested gently on the bars. Brake and clutch levers should be angled downwards, in such a way that when the arms are in the position described, stretching out one's fingers will bring them just above the levers. The hand grips on the bars themselves should be either level, or angled slightly downwards, for optimum control.

The footbrake, similarly, should be moved until it is just beneath the ball of the foot when you are seated in your normal riding position and wearing any foot covering you will normally don when on the machine.

Opinions differ, however, on the best position for the gearchange lever (Fig. 30). The more generally-accepted position for this is one which just permits the toe to slide beneath the pedal, though some riders prefer the toe to be above the pedal, and accept the disadvantage of a rather pronounced foot movement for downward changes. On balance, the former position seems best,

Fig. 30. Setting the gear control. Adjust footrest so that toe of foot is just above the gear lever in normal riding position. Match with footbrake on other side

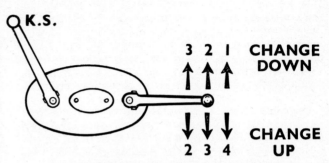

Fig. 31. Operation of motor cycle gear control
K.S.: Kick Start

since downward changes to assist braking need to be made more quickly than do upward changes.

On most motor cycles — although there are one or two well-known exceptions — the pedal is lifted to engage a lower gear and depressed to engage a higher (Fig. 31). Thanks to the inbuilt positive-stop mechanism, the pedal moves only sufficiently to engage one gear, and then returns to a central position.

To move off from a standstill, the clutch is disengaged, and the pedal raised with the toe to select first gear. Letting in the clutch gently, and opening the throttle as the drive begins to take up, ensures a smooth getaway. Second gear is engaged by closing the throttle, simultaneously pulling out the clutch. The gear pedal is then depressed as far as it will go to select second gear, the clutch released, and the throttle re-opened. Third gear — and fourth, too, if one is fitted — are selected in exactly the same manner.

To change down, momentarily close the throttle, operate the clutch, and lift the gear pedal with the toe, giving a quick "blip" on the throttle to help the gears engage. Release the clutch, and open the throttle, as soon as the gear is home.

Page twenty-five

It will be obvious from the preceding chapter that top gear is the one most generally used for cruising, but there is no virtue at all in making the engine "slog" in top gear when it would be far happier, and would work more efficiently, in one of the lower ratios. A novice should set himself to learn exactly which gear suits his engine best under any given set of circumstances, and to use the gearbox accordingly.

Once the knack of gearchanging on a motor cycle has been mastered it is a never-ending source of delight, and the skilful motor cyclist makes full use of the delicate control which mastery of the gearbox gives him. There is a saying that "the gearbox is the best brake", and under many conditions this is true. Emergency stops apart, it is always best to use the gearbox when slowing, dropping through the gears at the appropriate times, with the throttle closed, to lose speed against the compression of the engine. This is known as braking "on the over-run", and the brakes themselves are used only to "kill" the last few miles per hour.

Of the two brakes, the front is the more important. Many newcomers fail to realise this — possibly as the result of a "hangover" from cycling days — and often leave it unused.

In actual fact, it is not only a more powerful brake than the rear, but also a safer brake. When the front brake is applied, the machine's weight is transferred forward, pressing the tyre on to the ground and giving enhanced road grip. No such beneficial weight transference happens when the rear brake is used, and thus braking distances are longer when this alone is applied.

For maximum braking power, the front brake should be applied a split second before the rear brake. Initial application should be gentle, but as soon as the machine begins to lose speed — and there is usually only another split second to wait before this happens — pressure on both brakes should be steadily increased, until the model comes to a standstill with both brakes hard on. If a skid starts to develop, the brakes can be momentarily released, and then re-applied.

To slow for corners, it is usual to rely upon a gentle touch on the front brake, allied with selection of the appropriate lower gear. Where the roads are wet or icy, as much braking as possible should be accomplished on the gearbox, and the brakes used very gingerly, if at all.

To corner a motor cycle, it is simply leaned to one side or the other. That, at any rate, is the simple way of looking at it. Actually, of course, there is far more to it than that, but only road experience can teach the novice the finer points of cornering. The secret is simple, but exacting — to arrive at the corner at the right speed, in the right position on the road, in the right gear. After that, the corner itself is a mere formality. It is the correct judgment of the approach which really matters.

As a general rule, a left-hand corner should be approached with the machine slowing down in third, or possibly even second, gear, and positioned about one quarter of the way out across the road. Speed should be adjusted, if necessary, by a touch of front brake as the corner approaches. The machine is then leaned to the left and the throttle opened very gently to accelerate the machine around. As it comes through the corner it is gradually brought upright, and the higher gears are engaged once this process has been completed.

A right-hand bend is a trickier proposition, owing to the adverse road camber. The actual approach is the same, though the machine should be nearer the centre of the road than for a left-hander. In both cases, however, it is advisable to eschew braking or changing gear when the machine is actually banked over.

Sidecar Driving

Sidecar driving is an art in itself. Despite its assymetric layout, with the power, weight and braking concentrated on one side of the centre line of the vehicle, the sidecar outfit is one of the safest types of machine on the road, and even its foibles can be turned to good account.

With a sidecar fitted on the left, the outfit will have certain fixed tendencies. On a sharp left turn, the sidecar wheel will tend to come into the air (Fig. 32a). On a right hand bend, the rear wheel of the machine can be lifted by clumsy handling (Fig. 32b). To obviate these tendencies, the sidecar driver will accelerate on left-handers, and apply the motor cycle brakes on right-handers. These actions bring out-of-balance forces back into equilibrium.

The great feature of the sidecar outfit is that it is practically skid-proof. Given correct alignment of the sidecar, the outfit is virtually self-correcting. If, on an

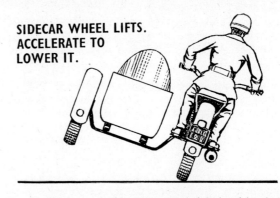

SIDECAR WHEEL LIFTS. ACCELERATE TO LOWER IT.

Fig. 32. Sidecar on left-hand bend and right-hand bend: *Fig.* 32a (*above*) Effect of failure to accelerate on left-hand bend and/or too much turn of front wheel. *Fig.* 32b (*below*) Effect of excessive speed on right-hand bend. Loss of control almost complete.

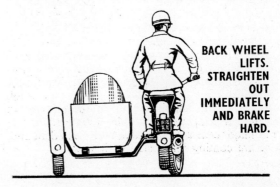

BACK WHEEL LIFTS. STRAIGHTEN OUT IMMEDIATELY AND BRAKE HARD.

icy road, the machine tries to slide to one side or the other, the free-rolling sidecar wheel acts as a castor, and tries to push it back. The result is a vehicle of truly remarkable stability.

Most learner-drivers who tackle a sidecar fail to realise that when the motor cycle brakes are applied the effect is to swing the machine to the right. When braking a sidecar outfit, unless it has a coupled sidecar brake, it is always necessary to steer slightly left as the brakes go on.

Only a few years back there existed no organisation which could help the motor cycle novice to reach proficiency. Now there exists an excellent scheme — the RAC/A-CU Training Scheme — in which, for a nominal fee, a learner is given tuition by experts, on private ground and on public roads, and is tested beyond the Ministry of Transport Driving Test standard before receiving a Proficiency Certificate. Instruction is also given in the theory and maintenance of motor cycles and scooters. The Proficiency Certificate does not absolve a rider from taking the M.o.T. Test, but it is a tangible sign that his novitiate is a thing of the past. The Motor Cycle Manager, Royal Automobile Club, Pall Mall, London, S.W.1, will supply details of the scheme on request. Though not yet countrywide, it is operated at a number of major centres in England, Wales and Scotland, and more are coming into being each year.

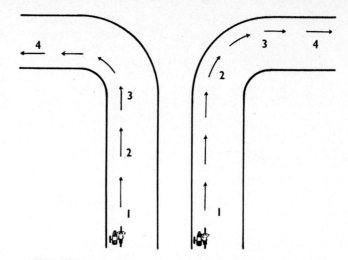

ABOVE LEFT

Fig. 33a. Left-hand bend with a sidecar:
1. Close throttle, change down, and lose speed on the "over-run".
2. Adjust speed with the brakes.
3. Be at correct speed by this point. Open throttle, gently press bars to accelerate around bend.
4. Re-engage top gear.

ABOVE RIGHT

Fig. 33b. Right-hand bend with sidecar:
1. Close throttle, and change down if necessary.
2. Slightly apply brakes.
4. Release brakes and accelerate.
3. Re-engage top gear.

MOTOR CYCLIST'S WORKSHOP

IT IS ALMOST a tradition in the motor cycle movement that the motor cyclist is also an amateur mechanic. The "Do-it-yourself" cult was anticipated by motor cyclists many years ago! There is much to commend this attitude. The rider who works on his own machine soon gets to know it inside out, and can answer for its condition at any moment. Knowing exactly what makes it tick, he is also a better rider in consequence.

Naturally, motor cycle maintenance is something which has to be learned. The RAC/A-CU course, outlined in the previous chapter, helps to teach the basic technique. Many local Evening Institutes include courses on the broad subject of vehicle maintenance, and the number of informative handbooks published on both general aspects and individual machines runs into scores, if not hundreds.

Even so, none of this is a substitute for getting out the tools and actually doing a job on one's own machine. The first essential is to have somewhere to work; the second to have the tools; the third to have ample time for the planned job.

Ideally, one should have a small workshop (Fig. 34), or at least a bench in the garage. If the machine can be mounted on a ramp, so much the better, since it makes for easier working. Suitable types are sold commercially, but it is a fairly easy job to construct one oneself out of stout timber, with a metal or plastics covering to the working top.

A minimum tool kit would consist of a set of open-ended spanners; a set of rings and boxes; two or three sizes of screwdriver, including a small one for electrical work; a pair of pliers with strong wire-cutters; a vice; a hammer, soft-metal drift, and cold chisel; a hacksaw; a couple of files; a scraper (which can be made by sharpening a piece of hardwood or filing an edge on a stick of solder); and a soldering iron. With this as a basis, and with any special service tools which the particular motor cycle or scooter requires, almost any job can be tackled. Continental machines, of course, will require sets of metric spanners.

Extra equipment needed can often be improvised from household goods or jetsam found in the garden shed. Some clean boxes in which to place parts removed from the machine are one requirement; a couple of baking tins to receive drained oil and to contain petrol or paraffin for washing dismantled components are another. Any rag used should be non-fluffy, and it is normally better to use a good-quality paintbrush for this work.

Discarded tins can be usefully employed to hold spare nuts and bolts. Jam jars come in handy for the same purpose. And an excellent washing bath for larger items can be made by cutting open an old oil drum, obtainable from a garage for a few shillings.

In the workshop itself, tools should be hung from hooks or nails driven into the walls, assuming that a proper tool cabinet is not available. Tins and jars should be labelled, and all rubbish put immediately into a waste tin — which can be a discarded oil drum with the top removed.

Extra equipment can be added piecemeal. A power

Fig. 34. Layout for a small workshop

drill is an invaluable tool, and it can be used to power a small lathe if necessary, as well as providing the basis for a grinding wheel, buffer, wire wheel and so forth For ease of working, an inspection light on a long lead is invaluable, and the workshop should be as well lighted as possible as a general rule. Fluorescent strips give a more even illumination than filament bulbs, and should be installed wherever possible.

Finally, if engines are to be run in the workshop it is important to remember that adequate ventilation should be provided, since exhaust fumes contain poisonous carbon monoxide gas.

Fig. 35. Touring in Kent   K. G. Jones

MOTOR CYCLE TOURING

BY ITS VERY nature, the two-wheeler is the touring vehicle par excellence. It is capable of tackling rough roads far more easily than can a car, and thus allows a much wider choice of touring area. It is economical enough to make long-distance tours a practical proposition, even on a limited budget, and it allows the rider to feel in touch with the countryside and to savour its air, rather than being a rather detached observer in transit through it.

Even the smallest motor cycle — or a moped, for that matter — can be used for touring. The sole requirements are a set of panniers to enable enough personal luggage to be carried, though a tour will obviously be more comfortable if some degree of weather-protection is also added to the machine.

Before setting out on a tour, the machine should be thoroughly checked and any doubtful items replaced. It is a good idea to decarbonise about 14 days before the tour is due to start, to enable the engine to settle down nicely before tackling what may, after all, be a fortnight of concentrated hard work.

It is a good idea too, to become a motor cycle member of one of the motoring organisations — the A.A. or the R.A.C.— so that in the event of trouble you can call upon their extensive and expert services. This is particularly necessary if it is foreign touring which is contemplated.

For this, you will need certain vehicle documents — either a carnet, which the motoring organisations issue, or a customs declaration form. The carnet costs more but carries with it free port services, for which the user of a declaration form may have to pay independently. A special green card issued by an insurance company to extend cover to use outside the British Isles is also necessary, and the driver must be the holder of a full driving licence. The one exception is in the case of a moped, when the country which is to be visited does not require a moped rider to hold any form of licence.

The motoring organisations can be of assistance in home touring too, for they will plan routes and provide touring information for any member who requires it.

In Scotland, motor cyclists are able to make use of youth hostels, which is an excellent way of cutting tour costs. Unfortunately the English youth hostels are less enlightened than are their opposite numbers in Scotland and the Continent, and bar motorists of all types.

When planning a tour, it is best to allow plenty of time for sightseeing, meals and so forth and to be generous in the running time allowed for each stage. Only 100 miles covered in a day's ride adds up to a fortnight's tour of some 1,500 miles. Thus it is advisable never to budget on exceeding 150 miles in a day's run. The situation is different, of course, where the plan is to ride direct to a specific area, and to tour there extensively. Under these conditions, up to 300 miles could easily be covered in a day on even the smallest machine on the outward trip, though rather more time should be allowed on the return, to take care of unforeseen snags.

Other facets of motor cycle touring are to combine it with camping, carrying a light tent and simple camping gear, or by towing one of the specially-designed light caravans behind a combination. When this is done, of course, a 30 m.p.h. maximum speed limit applies.

These two types of motor cycle touring are perhaps the most satisfying — and certainly the cheapest. Motor cycle campers or caravanners, however, should always be careful to ensure that the land on which they decide to stop for the night is not private. If it is, most farmers and land-owners will readily give permission for it to be used, so long as no damage is done and the site is left tidy.

MOTOR CYCLE CLUBS
and THE A.-C.U.

ALTHOUGH MOTOR CYCLING, in any of its aspects, is an enjoyable hobby, to obtain the utmost enjoyment from it the newcomer should join a club. In Britain the club movement forms the backbone of motor cycling. All motor cycle sport, save for the commercialised speedway and a few unimportant freelance events, is organised by the clubs. A few of these events are open to unattached riders, but the great majority call for club membership as a condition of entry. This point apart, the clubs have much to offer in the way of social events — dances, dinners, film shows, organised weekend runs, factory visits and so forth — which are in themselves well worth the purely nominal subscriptions which most clubs charge.

Co-ordinating and controlling the club movement is the governing body of English, Welsh and Scottish motor cycle sport, the Auto-Cycle Union. Founded in 1903, as a branch of the Royal Automobile Club, the A.-C.U. can now claim more than 800 clubs in its membership, spread over the 20 centres which cover England and Wales. Scotland has a separate National club in the Scottish A.-C.U., while Ireland has its own controlling organisation — the Motor Cycle Union of Ireland.

The A.-C.U. is a democratic body. It is governed by a General Council, consisting of representatives drawn from every Centre. The Centres are themselves managed by delegates elected from all constituent clubs. The result is that the A.-C.U. General Council has the benefit of the experience of men, from every part of the country, who are either practising motor cyclists themselves, or whose love of the game has kept them within the club ranks when their competition days are over.

Besides the Centres, various other bodies are represented on the General Council. There are certain clubs — such as the British Motor Cycle Racing Club and the Vintage Motor Cycle Club — whose interests are countrywide, and which would obviously not be able to fit into the purely regional grouping provided by Centres. Such clubs affiliate direct to the Union, and are represented on the Council. So, too, are the national clubs of the Commonwealth, which control the sport in Australia, New Zealand, Ceylon, Malaya, Northern and Southern Rhodesia, East Africa and Singapore.

The day to day administration is delegated by the General Council to two main committees — the Management Committee and the Competitions Committee. "Competition", of course, is a wide field, and to ensure the utmost efficiency in planning and administration, the Competitions Committee itself has nine standing sub-

K. G. Jones

Fig. 36. One of the benefits conferred by club life is the opportunity
to learn from experts.

committees dealing with the most important branches and aspects of the sport. Finally, the executive work is done by a small, but devoted, full-time headquarters staff in the A.-C.U. offices in Pall Mall, London.

Besides controlling and administering, the A.-C.U. has another very important duty to perform — the organisation of certain highly important sporting events. Pride of place, of course, goes to the Tourist Trophy

Races, an international event held every June in the Isle of Man. Generally acknowledged as the world's premier road race — and, consequently, justifying a separate chapter in this booklet — the T.T. calls for the most careful and painstaking planning, and for equal care in the execution of the plans once they are made. This annual challenge the A.-C.U. accepts, and meets to such purpose that the Tourist Trophy always sets a standard for organisation which is the envy of the world.

Other annual events which the A.-C.U. organises itself — or which are organised on its behalf by a member club or Centre — are an international road race meeting on August Bank Holiday; the Inter-Centre Team Championship Trial; the National Grass Track Championships; an Inter-Centre Team Championship Scramble; the International Moto Cross Grand Prix of Britain; the 250 c.c. International Moto Cross Grand Prix, and the National Rally. On occasions the A.-C.U. also organises, on behalf of the F.I.M. (the Federation Internationale Motocycliste), the International Six Days' Trial, Moto Cross des Nations and the Trophee des Nations.

Yet another facet of the Union's work is in maintaining a homogenous standard of time-keeping for race meetings and other events where the time factor enters into the picture. It does so by approving time-keepers — the men who, with great dexterity, handle highly accurate stop-watches to the fine limits demanded by current racing speeds. Four "grades" are recognised, and a separate register is compiled of timekeepers for speedway meetings.

Officials from the A.-C.U. also "vet" and measure new courses; check machines and equipment; and act as stewards at sporting events. Work for the movement on these lines is, in fact, often the postscript to a distinguished riding career, and the list of A.-C.U. committee members and timekeepers contains many names which would have been familiar to followers of racing or trials a decade or more ago.

Besides its endeavours for motor cycle sport in this country, the A.-C.U. also plays its part in the wider field of international motor cycling. It represents Britain and the Commonwealth on the international governing body — the F.I.M. and A.-C.U. representatives serve on the various Committees maintained by the international body.

Forming an individual branch of the Union is a comparatively new body, the National Scooter Association, which caters for the growing number of enthusiasts for this more specialised form of two-wheeler. The N.S.A. too, is organised through regional centres, of which 11 have been formed.

All this, however, has its real basis in the local clubman. The club movement has never before been so strong, nor so influential, and there is real pride to be gained as well as tangible advantages, from membership of a body with such a proud record of service and progress.

STANDARD MACHINE SPORT

ALTHOUGH FOR the specialised side of motor cycle sport, which will be dealt with later in the book, it is necessary to possess a motor cycle expressly designed for the job, there is much one can do with a standard production motor cycle.

Ninety per cent. of the club riders in this country have standard machines. Clubs make a corresponding effort to provide sport for them, and they make the events as attractive as possible by including a social element as well, although some of the rallies — for example, the Isle of Man International Scooter Rally or the Rossendale Enduro — are tough tests of driving skill and perseverance, as are the long-established M.C.C. trials, such as the Land's End Trial.

Every Sunday afternoon, however, one can find a club which has organised some more light-hearted competition. Treasure hunts are highly popular, and are run principally over main roads, though occasionally fairly easy farm tracks or moorland paths are included. The idea is to locate the "treasure" from a series of clues or map references. Organisers plan these events with one eye on the scenic value of the route, and since most end with a tea and a social evening the treasure hunt is a popular excursion with the passengers as well.

Main road trials are on similar lines, save that in many cases accurate time-keeping enters into the matter. Each rider has to cover the distance between set check-points at a set average speed, marks being lost for early or late arrival. To help decide ties, some special tests are normally included. Zig-zagging between markers; an acceleration and braking test; various other machine-control tests — these provide a useful method of eliminating competitors and serve a useful purpose in helping to improve one's machine handling.

Rallies often tend to be tougher propositions. They may involve some hundreds of miles of riding, with the emphasis on split-second timekeeping to maintain the exact specified average speed between check points, while the elimination tests are designed to be as difficult as possible, since the actual road section may have been successfully completed by several score competitors. The major British rally is that organised annually by the A.-C.U. — the National Rally. It terminates in a different town each year, and usually attracts around 1,000 entries, since besides being a fine test of a rider's ability it is also a great social gathering. The "possible" mileage which a rider can cover at the permitted average speed is normally no more than 650 miles in 24 hours riding. Each rider is free to plan his own route to take in the maximum number of controls or merely to visit a minimum on his way to the rally centre. Of course, such a rider won't win the premier award, but he will probably enjoy his weekend despite that!

Standard machine trials come into a very different class of sport, which is often held on private ground. Trials — or reliability trials, to give them their full name — will be more fully explained in the next chapter.

They consist of tackling rough ground not at speed, but in such a way that the rider uses his feet to steady himself as seldom as possible. Marks are lost for "footing" or stopping in observed sections of the course. In a standard machine trial, these sections are not normally very difficult. They may consist of paths strewn with rocks; steep climbs and descents on woodland paths; zig-zags marked out with tape; and so forth. The winner is the rider who loses fewest marks in these sections.

There are, of course, variations on these basic events. Some clubs might include a few observed sections in the course for a treasure hunt or map-reading contest; and there is another type of event which is sometimes included in a general programme — the *concours d'elegance* (Fig. 38).

This is a competition for the smartest and best-kept

Fig. 37. A typical scene at the start of a road trial.

K. G. Jones

Fig. 38. Concours d'Elegance

motor cycle .. and that does not necessarily mean the motor cycle displaying the greatest area of chromium plate. Judges at a concours — at club level, anyway — look for other signs of pride of ownership, such as "unrounded" nut and bolt heads, and take into account such factors as the age of the machine and the amount of work the owner himself has obviously put into its preparation. The concours has great attractions, more especially if other clubs are invited to take part, since the enthusiast has the opportunity to inspect the competing machines, and to glean ideas from them which he can apply to his own. Often, too, some interesting motor cycles are entered — older models, maybe, or even a "special" built from various makes of component by the competitor himself.

Though standard machines are employed in it, a gymkhana is a rather specialised form of event — virtually a show of motor cycle riding and control. The high spots, of course, are the exhibition pieces performed by skilled riders, but free-for-all events are usually included in the form of obstacle races and so forth. A moto-ball match — football on motor cycles — is often included in the programme. This is an old branch of the sport which is gaining popularity, but it is hardly the place for standard machines!

SPEED EVENTS and TRIALS

Road Racing

OF ALL MOTOR cycle sport, it is undoubtedly racing which most captures the imagination, and road racing above all. There is a stirring atmosphere about a motor cycle race, with the helmeted and leather-clad riders crouched over their fast machines, each seeking the slight advantage in position or tactics which will bring him victory. There is joy in the sight of a top-liner sweeping majestically through corners, on just the right "line" — and, perhaps passing two or three slower men with a superb display of riding. Even the machines themselves are the epitome of power — stripped of every superfluous component; lithe; powerful — and in beautiful condition.

Motor cycle racing starts in the workshop. Save in certain chosen events where factory-prepared machines are competing, the machines on the track are over-the-counter racing models of fairly standard design. By careful tuning and assembly, individual enthusiasts strive to obtain just that extra atom of performance which may make all the difference between a win or a "place". Sometimes, gifted engineers specialise in such work.

Occasionally, too, a rider will design and build his own machine, perhaps "marrying" components produced by several manufacturers with some of his own devising to produce a "special". Machines so conceived have often proved highly successful.

During race practice, the rider has two jobs on hand.

One is to learn the circuit, weighing up the various corners, and deciding how best to tackle them. At the same time, he is fitting his machine to the course, and deciding whether a slightly bigger jet in the carburettor, or a change in the overall gearing, will give him better times.

In the race itself he has only one object — to be first across the finishing line. He will not normally be concerned with trying to snatch a lap or race record, unless the speed of the race is such that he is forced to do so. Most riders sensibly believe that a race should be won as slowly as possible!

Great importance attaches to the start. The riders and their machines line up across the track, or in depth on a starting grid. Actual positions may be allocated on the basis of times in practice, or as a result of a ballot. The starter holds aloft a Union Jack, and then brings it down. This is the signal to start. Immediately, the riders run with their machines, letting home the clutches as quickly as possible to "bump start" the powerful engines. As soon as the engine fires, the rider jumps aboard, and is away.

Actual race tactics vary from circuit to circuit, and from rider to rider. There are some famous racing men who always prefer to race from behind, sitting close behind the leader and letting him set the pace, only to streak past him at the last moment. Others are uncomfortable when they are forced to follow another rider, and prefer to go to the front at once, and then, with a clear road ahead, set a pace which will suit them-

B. R. Nicholls

Fig. 39. Sidecar racing is a favourite sport with the crowds; it is spectacular, and requires a split-second co-ordination between the driver and his passenger. By shifting his weight, the passenger stabilises the outfit on corners.

selves. That great rider Mike Hailwood is an outstanding example of this school; and is, in addition, one of the most meteoric riders off the mark of post-war years.

Once the race is under way, riders soon sort themselves out into groups. A man with a slower machine will often be able to hold a faster man by "slip-streaming" — tucking close in behind, so that he is riding in the vortex created by the machine in front. Having less air resistance to overcome, the machine behind gains in speed, and its driver's object will be to hold this position as long as possible, thus taking any opportunity of slipping by which occurs once the time is right for such a manoeuvre. The man in front however, is aware of this, and *his* aim will be to lose his pursuer, either by stepping up the pace, or by out-riding him on the corners.

The tactic of riding from behind is also sometimes used by a man with a relatively slow but reliable machine to "push" a rider whose machine is faster, but fragile. By so dictating the pace, the slower man hopes that the other machine will have to be driven beyond its margin of reliability and will, as they say, "blow up". Calculations such as this, of course, are commoner in Grand Prix racing than in the more limited field of everyday road racing, but nonetheless it is the man who races with his head who wins with the least expenditure of effort and the least strain on his machine.

Sidecar racing is, perhaps, the favourite of the spectators. Racing sidecars are very sparse affairs — usually merely a chassis; a platform; and a streamlined nose.

To help in cornering, the passenger leans well out to the left on left-handers, and places his weight over the rear wheel on right-handers. Driver and passenger work together as a team to keep the outfit moving fast and in the right direction, and it is perhaps this teamwork which gives this branch of the sport its fascination.

Grasstrack racing is one of the most popular and widely-spread of the speed sports. Courses, which may be plain ovals or twisting "semi-road" tracks, are laid out in suitable fields. They may be very short — perhaps less than half a mile — and are very rarely of more than a mile in length. The type of machine used, and the tactics employed, vary from Centre to Centre. Some grass-track meetings are simply speedways on grass, with riders broadsiding round on spindly speedway mounts. Others may attract "specials" which would not look seriously out of place on a short road circuit, and here a variant of road-racing style may predominate.

Grass-track racing tends to be a more social type of sport than road racing, with spectators closer to the racing itself and more easily able to wander round to inspect the various machines.

For both road and grass, riders are obliged to wear protective clothing, consisting of a riding suit of horsehide, suitably padded at vulnerable points, a crash helmet, gloves, and a pair of leather boots. Sidecar passengers must have the same equipment, but are allowed plimsolls to give a better grip on the swaying platform of the sidecar.

Scrambles

The third type of racing is scrambling, or moto-cross. It is spectacular, and an outstanding test of skill in the rider and stamina in the machine. A scramble is a race across country, a course being laid out on rough ground and paths. It will usually include steep climbs and descents, and may have mud and water as an extra hazard. Machines, here, are usually special scrambles mounts designed for the job by a factory, though there are some highly successful "specials" as well. Speeds, as might be expected, are relatively low. It is unusual for an average speed to be higher than 30/35 m.p.h., and on many courses it may even be below this. For this reason, it is a very even sport, in which the smaller-engined, lighter machine stands as good a chance as the bigger mount.

As a spectacle, the scramble is supreme. The bucking and bouncing of the machines; breathtaking leaps; full-bore climbs of slippery banks; all these would be awe-inspiring in themselves, even without the added suspense provided by the competitive element.

Trials

But the clubman's sport is trials riding — for the very good reason that this is a branch of the game in which almost any rider can compete, and in which age is no bar. A reliability trial is a supreme test of the rider's ability to control his machine under any conditions. The yardsticks are observed sections, which are often of

B. R. Nicholls

Fig. 40. Scrambling — racing across country — is a tough sport, which imposes great strain on both rider and machine.

almost incredible ingenuity, and great difficulty — though this depends, to some extent, upon the status of the trial.

There are certain sections which are old favourites, included regularly in national events. But for every one of these there are hundreds of local "stoppers", up and down the country, which test the wits of scores of ordinary clubmen. Speed plays no part in a trial, save that a set time is normally allowed for the completion of the course. Sections may be situated close together, or separated by miles of open road. The course is planned, and marked. Riders set off individually from the start, usually at minute or half-minute intervals; sometimes in groups, where the entry runs into several hundreds. Each rider tackles a section alone, and an observer notes his performance. If his machine stops in the observed section, he is debited five marks. If he has to use his feet to steady himself, or to keep in motion, he loses three; if he rides through unaided, he loses none. Sometimes, a single "dab" to maintain balance is scored less severely than persistent footing.

At the end of the day, all the observers' cards are checked, and the marks lost by each rider totalled. The man who has lost fewest marks is the winner, and ties are settled in various ways — by means of a special test, or by the distance covered before marks were lost, or by some equally fair means.

Normally, there are premier and capacity class awards to be won by the best performers, and all who come within a certain percentage of the winner's total receive first-, second- or third-class awards. It is unusual for the

K. G. Jones

Fig. 41. A tough section! Trials riding calls for immaculate machine control, but even the best riders have to foot sometimes to keep their machines on the move.

prizes to be of great value, for with trials riding the sport is the main consideration.

Trials motor cycles, of course, are specialised machines. They have to cope with a great variety of conditions, for sections may consist of mud, sand, water, rocks, chalk — any hazard which the astute trials organiser thinks may baffle competitors. *His* aim is to find a section which is *almost* impossible. If each section was ridden clean by only one man, and that man was a different rider on each section, the organiser would feel that he had selected a perfect course. Besides coping with all types of rough surfaces, the trials machine must also, however, be road-worthy, so that it can be used on public roads between sections, and can also be ridden to events.

For this reason, they are usually special versions of catalogued touring machines. Ground clearances are increased, footrest widths reduced, greater movement given to the steering, and the weight is cut. But they are still road-going motor cycles, and many enthusiastic clubmen use their machines as daily transport, and ride them in events at weekends. Trials riding is therefore a sport which is within the financial reach of anybody who can afford to buy a motor cycle, and since there are plenty of events in which to ride it is a side of the hobby which can be enjoyed all the year round.

Other types of motor cycle event include sprints — virtually acceleration matches over a measured distance; hill climbs, in which a steep (and sometimes highly tricky) hill is tackled at speed; and, for the elite, the tough multi-day trials.

Chief of these is the Scottish Six-day Trial, with observed sections and time schedules to meet. This annual event takes place in the Highlands, and forms a sporting holiday for real enthusiasts, who welcome the tough opposition and the formidable challenge of the mountain sections.

The International Six-day Trial is rather different, being more on the lines of a cross-country race. This event is perhaps the most important single event in the international motor cycling calendar, after the T.T. Races, and competition within it is of the highest calibre. Each class of motor cycle has a set schedule to maintain — a schedule which leaves very little room for mistakes. The going is extremely tough. In addition parts of the motor cycle itself are "sealed", and failure of one of these parts to operate properly at the daily inspection means disqualification. The I.S.D.T. is more the preserve of national and manufacturers' teams than of the private owner, but some super-enthusiasts do, in fact, compete with success.

In motor cycle sport generally, classification is by the cubic capacity of the engine. It is rare, in racing, to find machines permitted to race out of their category, but in the trials world the top prizes are open to all comers. Small two-strokes have won almost every major British trial, and teams of lightweights have done well in the I.S.D.T.

THE TOURIST TROPHY RACES

AT FIRST SIGHT it may seem a little odd that the world's premier road race should be called the "Tourist Trophy", but this fact reflects the purpose for which it was instituted, by far-sighted pioneers, in 1907.

Their object was to perfect the touring motor cycle through the supreme test of racing, and through the years the T.T. Race has done just that, and done it more effectively than any other method.

Since 1911, the T.T. has been run over the famous 37.735 mile "Mountain" course in the Isle of Man. The Island was chosen as the venue because there alone was it possible to close public roads for a period, to enable the races to be run. After four races over the original "short" course, the move to the Mountain was decided upon to provide the toughest test of all. It has classes for 50 c.c., 125 c.c. (Ultra lightweight), 250 c.c. (Lightweight), 350 c.c. (Junior) and 500 c.c. (Senior) solos and for Sidecars.

The Isle of Man Course stands supreme as an all-round test of machine and rider. Other courses, notably the ultra-fast Continental tracks such as that for the Belgian Grand Prix at Spa, may be harder on certain parts of the machine, but no one course can provide such a variety of conditions as can the Island. Furthermore, it is the supreme test of a rider. Its numerous corners, gradients and curves are a perpetual challenge to the motor cyclist's skill, and it is doubtful whether even the greatest riders have ever yet produced a *perfect* lap of this famous circuit.

For many years the T.T. was the great testing ground for the whole British motor cycle industry. Often enough, the machines raced there one year would form the basis for the following year's new production models. As speeds rose, however, this form of direct development was no longer practical, and the number of manufacturers competing shrank. The machines themselves, too, became specialised racing models, but the central purpose — that of developing the motor cycle — has never been undermined. In recent years the development of efficient rear suspension is a direct result of racing practice. One manufacturer has frames on his standard models which were first developed, and tested, in the T.T. Races. Another has a gearbox which was first tested in precisely the same way. Better brakes; better handling; even better weather protection — first tested as racing streamlining — have resulted from this great road-racing contest.

Unlike the majority of road events, the T.T. is not a massed-start race. There are too many hazards to make that a practical proposition. For many years, riders set out, one by one, at intervals — rather in the manner of a cycling time trial — and were racing the clock, rather than each other. Now, they start in pairs, but the differential timing still exists. To keep track of the race, the spectators at the starting line have the aid of a gigantic scoring board, on which each rider's growing times are shown lap by lap, and a leader-board listing the placings of the leading six riders.

To help them weigh up their positions, the riders themselves establish unofficial "signal stations" on the course, where a helper can indicate, by means of a blackboard and code just how the rider is faring. Tactics play a great part in T.T. racing, where one may often not even see the opposing riders.

The race itself is, however, only the culmination of weeks of planning and work. On the organisation side, the A.-C.U. — with fifty years' experience behind it — faces this annual undertaking with confidence. Practising facilities have to be arranged; entries checked; all the hundred-and-one problems of organising an event which will spread, including practising, over a fortnight have to be faced and solved. For the riders, the weeks before the T.T. mean careful hours spent preparing machines and transport; arranging accommodation; helpers; fuel; spares and so forth.

Practising presents a special problem. Obviously, the work of the Isle of Man cannot be completely disrupted every day, so practising normally takes place at sunrise, or in the evening. The conditions, therefore, are not exactly the same as will pertain during the race. The morning air is cold and heavy; the evening air usually warm. Carburation differs in both circumstances, and differs again in the race itself, which is run around mid-day, so far as the Junior and Senior events are concerned.

Riders therefore have to weigh up all the factors, and decide their various engine settings from the permutations they achieve. They have to "guesstimate" their gearing, too — half a tooth more or less in the overall gearing between engine and wheel may mean a better

Fig. 42. George Meier   *Motor Cycle*

Fig. 43. Mike Hailwood   *B. R. Nicholls*

climb of the thousand-foot Mountain, or a quicker run along the mile-long Sulby Straight. Both factors will have an effect on fuel consumption, and the timing of the pit stop for refuelling may be a critical factor in winning, or losing, the race.

Year by year, speeds in the T.T. have been growing — save where the weather has intervened. In 1939, Georg Meier (Fig. 42) on a 500 c.c. supercharged B.M.W., set a record speed of 89.38 m.p.h. This was surpassed by Geoff. Duke — one of the greatest riders the Island has seen — in 1950, when on an unsupercharged Norton he averaged 92.27 m.p.h.

History was made, two-fold, in the 1960 T.T. races. Riding his bi M.V. Agusta "four", John Surtees became the first rider ever to win a T.T. race at a speed of over 100 m.p.h., and the first ever to win three Senior T.T. races in succession.

Only gearbox trouble, which struck when he was leading the Junior event, robbed him of the distinction of a "double treble" or winning three Senior *and* Junior T.T.'s in succession.

In recent years Mike Hailwood (Fig. 43) has dominated the T.T. scene. He won three T.T.'s in 1961, the first rider ever to score a "triple", and since then he has scored single wins in 1962, 1963 and 1964.

The T.T. is one of those major races which count for the F.I.M. World Championship. Riders, in each capacity class, score points in these races if they finish in the first six, the top-scoring rider at the end of the series being, of course, champion for the year in his capacity class.

LIVING HISTORY — THE VINTAGE MOVEMENT

ONE OF THE MOST fascinating aspects of the motor cycle game is to participate in its "living history" side. All over the country, enthusiasts seek out, buy and renovate examples of motor cycles of bygone days.

In this work, the Sunbeam M.C.C., which organises the annual Pioneer Run from Epsom to Brighton for pre-1915 machines, and the Vintage M.C.C., which caters for owners of pre-1931 machines, play a leading part.

The Pioneer Run, which is the highlight of the year for the "veteran" enthusiasts, was started by the Sunbeam club in the early '30s. After the war, with new motor cycles scarce, the Vintage movement gathered strength, and what had been at one time a rather light-hearted event became the annual parade for old motor cycles which, in many cases, had been renovated to showroom condition by enthusiastic owners.

To be eligible to compete in the Run, a machine must have been manufactured before December 31, 1914, and must comply with stringent rules regarding the originality of components. It must also be listed on the Pioneer Register — compiled by the Sunbeam club — which records details of every veteran machine recognised by the club as complying with the conditions. Only a few highly interesting machines are exempt from this requirement — the unique Vee-4 Douglas of 1908, for example. This engine is mounted in a standard 1913 Douglas frame, but being acknowledged to be of outstanding historic interest the hybrid model is allowed to compete.

The Pioneer Run is not a race. Machines are grouped in three classes, according to their age, and each class is given a strict time schedule. Early arrival at Brighton means disqualification. On an average, there are nearly 300 competitors, and this annual run — one of the most popular events in the motor cycling calendar — is a veritable pageant of the early history of the motor cycle manufacturing movement. British, French, German, Swiss, Belgian and American machines are among those competing, the earliest of them dating from the mid-1890s.

Wider in its scope, the Vintage club's Banbury Run caters for all machines built before 1931. The same high standards are maintained here as in the Brighton event. In addition, the Vintage club organises speed events, concours, section meetings and so forth, and publishes a fascinating monthly magazine.

For the individual enthusiast, the vintage cult is full

Fig. 44. Water cooling; a four cylinder engine; shaft drive; rear suspension — all were features of this 850 c.c. Wilkinson-T.M.C., built before the first World War.

K. G. Jones

Fig. 45. One manufacturer today is still using this layout—an inclined engine, acting as a front down tube—after 60 years. This particular example is a 1902 Humber. Despite their large engine early motor cycles approximated to to-day's mopeds in design and performance.

K. G. Jones

of interest. Unusual, and even famous, machines are found in unlikely places. A front-wheel drive Werner dating from about 1898, for example, was found in a ruined windmill. A Scott, bought " blind " from a scrap dealer for £1, proved to be one of the three "works" racers which had competed in the 1928 Senior T.T. Searching for machines like this in out-of-the way places gives weekend excursions a constructive object, and detective work — often based on a chance remark or even a "hunch" — is fascinating in itself.

The work of rebuilding, of course, calls for a sound mechanical knowledge, and for painstaking research. The correct colour schemes, types of lining, bright parts and so forth have all to be ascertained; obsolete components renovated; missing parts obtained or, at a pinch, manufactured. There is no more satisfying work for long winter evenings than bringing back to running order — or even to showroom condition — an example of a famous machine of yesteryear.